CW01212635

Dressing for the Afterlife

Dressing for the Afterlife

Maria Taylor

Nine
Arches
Press

Dressing for the Afterlife
Maria Taylor

ISBN: 978-1-913437-01-5
eISBN: 978-1-913437-02-2

Cover artwork: © Anthony Gerace
https://a-gerace.com

First published September 2020 by:

Nine Arches Press
Unit 14, Sir Frank Whittle Business Centre,
Great Central Way, Rugby.
CV21 3XH
United Kingdom

www.ninearchespress.com

Nine Arches Press is supported using public funding by Arts Council England.

Supported using public funding by
ARTS COUNCIL ENGLAND

Contents

Prologue

To dress for the afterlife,
step into the precise moment
you ended a former existence
and zipped yourself into the unknown.
Choose a wedding outfit,
a pair of overalls, an invisibility cloak,
or the national dress of a country
you have never visited before.
This is how you must learn
to breathe again.

She Ran

I took up running when I turned forty.
I opened my front door and started running
down a filthy jitty and past my parents' flat.
I ran through every town in which I'd ever lived.
I ran past all my exes, even a few crushes
who sipped mochas and wore dark glasses.
I ran in a wedding dress through scattered confetti
and was cheered by the cast of *Star Wars*.
I ran through the screaming wind, rain and cloud.
I ran through my mother's village and flew past
armed soldiers at the checkpoint. I ran past
my grandparents and Bappou's mangy goats
with their mad eyes and scaled yellow teeth.
I ran straight through Oxford and Cambridge,
didn't stop. I saw a naked man in Piccadilly Gardens.
I ran through high school and behind the gym
where gothy teens smoked and necked each other.
I passed an anxious mother pushing a pram
and a baby that kept throwing out her doll.
Seasons changed; summer turned into autumn,
I couldn't get as far as I wanted.
The lights changed. My ribs, my flaming heart
and my tired, tired body burned.

I Began the Twenty-Twenties as a Silent Film Goddess

On the first of January I threw away my Smartphone
and wrote a letter to my beau in swirling ink.
I bobbed my hair, wore a cloche hat and shimmied
right into town for Juleps. I became Clara.
I became Louise. When I became a vamp, the boys
fell dead at my feet, I threw petals over their heads.
I dined on prosperity sandwiches and sidecars,
leaving restaurants with a sugar-rimmed mouth.
In summer I was a night-blooming flower.
By autumn I was a hangover. Winter made me
a Wall-Street Crash. Talking pictures were my ruin.
At last I had a voice but no-one wanted to hear.
Forgotten sisters. Oh Vilma, oh Norma, oh Mae.
A musty headdress of peacock feathers. Defiant silence.

And there she was in the shrunken apartment like Joan Crawford, toy dog on her lap

But there's armour in glamour – a mirror's feisty glare of brow & lips – a shield of heavy floral scent – ardour in her gestures – waiting for the non-existent call – & stylish torpor on a sterile afternoon – amen to the small bronze men with 24 carat souls – they prop open doors where joy might cat-sneak in – the twentieth century invented the microwave for your solitary meals – hide Russian water in your flask – hear new and improved women read scripts meant for you – a memory of fat cigar-smelling fingers – brown trails on your porcelain neck – ghost of 'stick with me kid, I'll get you in the movies'– should it ring let the phone ring – let it ring – shut the bedroom door – we'll meditate on diamonds – our best friends – wear an expensive yoke from Tiffany's – remember Mae's words? – *hey Beulah, peel me a grape – there isn't any man in the world worth getting lines over* – a teardrop pendant sliding over heart or breast – depending on the beholder's eye.

The Floating Woman

i.m. Laura Stephen half-sister of Virginia Woolf

Sister, since I stopped
living for you I've heard of your passing.
You filled your pockets with stones
and returned to water.

I am much improved.
I don't spit or throw scissors into the fire
I don't stammer as I no longer speak
but I sing, sister.

When nurses bathe me
they pour rivers over my head.
I think of you, how every word
turned into water.

You wrote we were eight
though you never named me.
I am absent in our family portraits
but I am here.

Your lost footsteps echo.
I do not have a room, but corridors.
Walk here, sister. I will startle you
with my linen wings.

Sand Memoir

July is peculiar country   the view is long and ends in water
standing on the beach   I could be my own twin
I see myself butterfly   a lack of mermaid
my all-too-human toes   thrash at peaked waves
only sand and water   to clothe me
we stop at a café   eat *Kata-ifi,* but
the decor's changed   generations have shifted
my daughters demand pizza   order in perfect English

I am betraying the sun

I paid respects to the dead   saw church candles glow
now at the beach   the sun-tanned bask
in another solar system   they look through me

Then I Reconsidered Prayer

It was unlike me: light years since
my *Kyrie Eleison* or the cross
performed with three digits
over skull, stomach and shoulders.
In summer I went back to the chapel
in my father's austere village,
thinking it was ironic that St. Menas
resembled Frank O'Hara so perfectly.
I lit Frank a candle and prayed
at an altar of two-headed golden eagles
to our lady of infinite hangovers,
to the patron saint of Citalopram,
and the holy trinity of vodka, ageing
and insomnia. When the young priest
entered he was so kind that
I almost thought it was OK to be me;
if I kept quiet I could be part
of the stone. Once, a drunk
in a dingy Soho pub mistook
the moon I keep on a silver chain
around my neck for St. Christopher.
I told god about it. I lit another flame
for those who journey alone,
for the penitent and for the lost.

Aubade with Question Mark

How did it arrive –
through a door foolishly left open,
or as a reply to a lost note?
I awoke with a belief
I was searching in a forest
and followed you through a flicker
of aspen leaf and shadow.
You turned.
You were more than one man.
Lover. Enemy. Kin.
Dawn. Quarrel of birdsong.
On his daily round
the last milkman in England
clinks the empties.

Moon in Gemini

tonight the moon has two faces / happy sad

tonight the moon turns to its other / a twin in glass

tonight you'll show me constellations of ex-lovers / stolen light

tonight our eyes won't meet / tonight they will

tonight you'll think of the past / drown in neon

tonight a woman in a mirror says, 'go home' / don't listen

tonight be drunk & *very* wise / read: misguided

tonight you'll seek the moon / don't trust the brag

tonight someone will love / will hate

tonight the moon is frail / is strong

Everything is a fight between winter and spring

the sun burns lower   colder   a few dahlias refuse
to give up the gold of summer   liquidity of light
time is a tide of black water   see earth as a changing element
one that flows   observe a garden as a sundial in which
seasons are marked by shadows of shadows   and now
the heat goes but will return   the tide rises/ebbs through days
and years   and the earth will have its rot and bright colour
sunlight moves like water   over the year's continual end

Ophelia

He longs to pose her under a weeping tree,
and see her amber hair coil underwater.

He tracks desire with maps on his phone,
anywhere he catches the scent of her flowers.

Ophelia is his. Today she's a mystery.
He finds it impossible to capture her tint.

She's blocked him three times. He paints
over his errors with a cat-fished face.

He imagines kissing her open mouth,
Ophelia motionless in her beaded dress.

He paints grasses of yellow and Prussian blue
beyond her lifeless grasp. A floral noose

of withered violets, his artistic tributes
of poppies, forget-me-nots; her rigid hands.

He will tell her she was to blame,
the stagnant water so cold around her neck.

The Bee-Bird

We duly found an inscription under the base,
believed to be in Sir Vauncey's hand... We could
make out its name, 'the bee bird'... 'died 1895.'
– notes taken at Calke Abbey

In his cabinets of wasted wings
a heron's beak clasps a fish,
its convex eyes a jet prison.

Bell-jars of hoarded birds
stuffed with their master's tedium:
faded goldfinches and redpolls,
a frozen kestrel, wings unstretched
for impossible flight.

I imagine his birds reborn,
darting through his stuffy rooms,
a chaos of feathers in his Lady's boudoir,
across the airless library.

Unhatched eggs crack open.
Chicks beg, hungry for more
than sawdust and rags.

And there at his sash window
a yellow and black canary,
tiny and alive – singing, singing.

Awake in His Castle

I trespassed.
At night I found myself ice-skating
into someone else's life.
I felt a snowflake kiss my cheek
and saw statues of women
with weathered faces.

He thinks of me as a child.
I have a key for the room
where bodies move like spiders.
I sense the thump
of his heavy, grey heart.

My chamber is stone.
The door is oak.
The handle begins to turn.
I open it to prove nothing's there.

Ghosting

Think of Will, the ghost of Covent Garden,
the murdered thesp who's walking alongside you
down and down a staircase that never ends.

Dapper gent. Eventually you'll see daylight.
The actor won't. Spare a thought for the ghosts
we pass at stations: their secret meetings, flings, kisses.

People vanish into thin air every single day,
even ghosts fade in time. Where do they go
all those see-through Elizabethans,

Plantagenet kings in car parks, crying boys
reaching out for our faces, those we can't see, can't feel.
You're no different. Look, here's your own reflection.

Loop

Maybe time moves like a figure of eight,
surging forwards then back on itself.

Light returns from exploded stars.
A grown woman could turn a corner
and see herself crying as a girl.

Newsflash: our world ends again.
The disappearing forests of childhood
disappear again.
                                        The path curves.

It takes the woman back to a dimly-lit bar
where she meets the same lover again and again.
She risks everything once more.

They've already met
before they've said a word.

Dear Birthday

It's not the moon
I drink to tonight but Venus
shining like a fresh tear.
Look up. She's alone,
a celestial wallflower
outnumbered by stars.

Tonight I celebrate the uselessness
of dust motes and unwashed plates;
I celebrate unkempt gardens
and salute peonies
bent like sobbing, jilted brides.

I pour champagne into the wrong glass
and raise a tumbler to her clouds.
I'm celebrating everything being wrong.
Who cares that it's Tuesday?
Good stuff doesn't keep.

The Fields

From the train's mud-flecked window
you observe how the rain dissolves
a landscape you thought familiar.

Bulletins. Warnings. Rain stops play.
Why is it people lose their heads?
They pass by in flashes, their faces erased
by waterproofs and umbrellas.

Rain makes no apologies. A gate-crasher
at a wedding who drops hints
into fluted glasses. How the light alters.
The fields in flood. Signs. Road closed.

Reports show images of floating items,
a double bed, a car, an empty coffin.
You can't trace the fields on a map,
your place in this world an ever-shifting thing.

Head of a Baby

A sprinkle of veins:
blue, green, violet – the colours
of earth from space.

My fingers trace
the shape of a river.
Her fontanelle pulses
with heartbeats

    and so the water runs
    and so the water runs

Poem in Which I Lick Motherhood

I have several children, all perfect, with tongues made of soap and PVA glue running through their veins. My boys and girls benefit from eating the rainbow. I iron children twice daily. Creases are the devil's hoof-print. I am constructed from sticky-back tape, pipe cleaners and clothes pegs. There are instructions for making me. Look at the appropriate shelves in reputable stores. I am fascinated by bunk beds, headlice and cupcakes. You will only leave the table when I have given you clear instructions. So far I have not. The school-run is my red carpet. Yes, you're right, how *do* I manage it? Though, I didn't ask you. Dreaming is permitted from 7:40 to 8:20 am on Saturdays and Bank Holidays. My children's reward charts are full of glittery stars. I am the Milky Way. Crying is dirty. One housepoint! Two if you eat up all your peas. I always go off half an hour before my alarm. In the morning I speak a language of bleeps and bell tones. Chew with your mouth closed. No. Don't chew at all. Admire the presentation. Underneath my ribs is a complex weather system of sunshine and showers. Heat rises from me and blows across the gulf stream of my carefully controlled temper.

Sometimes I am mist.

What It Was Like

When the stranger's baby cries, my body remembers
the shrill, tuneless song of need. It remembers

endless nights of cat and dog rain. It remembers
our road falling asleep, as we forgot to remember us.

That summer, clothes stopped remembering
to fit. We'd look through thin curtains and remember

the sun, mimicked by sodium light. I remember
the feel of warm, sleep-suited limbs, still breathe in

their powdery smell. The stranger I used to be lives
in the present tense now. The baby fidgets on her chest

like a rabbit. Then he's calm. His blue eyes gnaw
on me for a moment till his head's at rest,

the frail, dreaming head of infancy that only knows
a need for love and milk, that won't remember any of this.

The Pavilion

Under the pavilion's eaves the year 1930 is carved.
They took pride in things when we had an empire,
one man's keen to tell me. Not that he would remember.
The empire has fallen like rotten teeth.

In that year Papou would've been twenty-five,
with less than twice that to live. How neat this building is,
how it reminds us of order and symmetry.
Papou would have known the same flag.

Men dressed in shrill whites play bowls.
One bowl bumps politely into another;
a soft ceramic chink, as if to say *excuse me,*
its manners rewarded with a round of applause.

When Papou died he was forty-seven.
No photographs. No letters.
He was handed down to me like a fairy tale
with no happy ending for his widow.

He'd had a stroke. The village had no doctors.
Yiayia rounded up chaos like a sheepdog
and raised six children. No time for pride.
Tea-time. The players head into the pavilion.

I stay outside.

Unfinished Business

Like the ghost who never realised
he was dead, or the unending record
stuck in a groove, or the comedian
who forgot the punchline, or the bud
spoiled by frost, or the last Rolo,
or the half-painted living room,
or Beethoven's draft of his tenth
chucked out by the cleaner,
or the bottle of fizz never opened
for a special day, or the rainy day
that rained all year. Who's sadder?
The man waiting at the bar,
or the woman who won't walk in?

Also-ran

That word made Babba angry
and curse the slack horses that didn't win.
Growing up I knew what it meant
but never felt its meaning,
till I stood behind you one day – invisible,
and overheard you say to a friend
you dreamed of her the night before.
The whip-crack of your tongue
buckled my knees ahead of the finish.

Babba, why didn't you look up
from the sports pages and warn me,
You can't compete with the ones they dream about.

Friday at The Moon

You're probably right, I look the type
who drinks vanilla lattes, but there I was
with a shot of something devastating,

and yes, I did entertain the regulars
with my slurred, cursive eloquence.
I probably sang. I probably chased a man

with a red rose between my teeth.
I tip-toed past the stone couple
who never talk to each other.

I tottered by Prosecco-fluted hens,
saluted the old boy in last season's mildew,
the Adidas man who speaks to his hands.

I saw pale ale ghosts. Lonely hearts.
Golf-kitted students necking snakebite
on a crawl they won't remember.

No idea how I got back, but if you said
I floated home on a magic carpet
who'd doubt it. I felt enchanted –

did I look happy to you?

Hypothetical

A friend of mine asks me if I'd sleep with Daniel Craig,
Before I have time to answer, I'm in bed with Daniel Craig.
He's stirring out of sleep, smelling of Tobacco Vanille,
he flatters my performance, asks if I'd like coffee.
'Hang on,' I say, 'I did not sleep with you, Daniel Craig,
this is just a conversational frolic.' My friend stands
in the corner of my bedroom. 'You've gone too far,' she says.
I'm pulling the duvet away from his Hollywood body
at exactly the moment my husband enters the room
I say, 'Yes, this is exactly what it looks like, darling,
but it's hypothetical, a mere conversational frolic.'
He's threatening me. There are lawyers in the room.
My children begin to cry. I don't even like Daniel Craig.

It's too late. The sheets are full of secreted evidence.
There are forensics in the room, covering my body
in blue powder, checking my skin for finger prints:
they match Daniel Craig's. He doesn't even know
he's slept with me. My marriage is a dead gull.
My neighbours come into the room shaking heads,
oh dear oh dear oh dear. My husband has drawn lists
of all the things he wants to keep: a plasma screen,
an X Box, a collection of muesli-coloured pebbles
from our holidays in Truro, 'When you loved me!'
he snaps. My children will see a therapist after school.

Daniel Craig is naked in a hypothetical sense,
telling me we can make this work. My friend smirks
behind a celebrity magazine featuring lurid details
of our affair. There are photos. We are on a beach
in the Dominican Republic, healthy and tanned
both kicking sand at a playful Joan Collins.

'I don't even *like* Daniel Craig,' I tell the ceiling.

Tracing Orion

You were already fully grown
and frolicking with lovers
under the stars, around the time
when I used my rough book
to trace constellations at night.
I'd recite names like magic spells:
Alnitak, Alnilam, Mintaka.
The hunter's body in space
impossible to touch.

You in the middle of nowhere
fumbling with straps in the dark.
Me in a box room. Star-gazing.

The Boyfriend

You envied my snakebite future
of liquored kisses in union bars,
saying even if love were impossible
could I feel sorry enough to kiss you?

Summer was up. My spine curled
into a question mark, a textbook rested
on my lap; bus rides to your house
brought on nausea – I'd jump out
before a bridge where cars vanished
over a steel-coloured horizon.

We shared tea and jam sandwiches,
looking through the window
of an eternal teenage bedroom.
Your mother was down in the garden
waving to us through metallic light.

The dogs bawled at her ankles,
her eyes were full of hope for me.

Learning to Love in Greek

They said beware *eros*, though many
begin with madness. Learn to fall
in love with dancing – this is *ludic,*
the love you felt for skipping ropes
or bikes. If *eros* and *ludus* combine
you may suffer *mania,* the white blood
of the moon that petrifies. Grow *phillia,*
the love of football fans on terraces.
Chant together. Fight with the same heart.

If you have children or a puppy
you'll know *storgi,* it rhymes with *be.*
It sits at kitchen tables, magnetises
crayon drawings to fridges. If you don't
have these, you may feel *storgi*
from an old aunt, a mate. A lover
might see the child hiding in you
from a cowlick of grey that won't
be brushed straight. Then *philautia,*
loving the self. Not so easy. For others,
who dive into pools of themselves,
too easy. Be your own best friend.
When love moves into a house
with a mortgage and enough space
for the future, this is *pragma.*
To *stand* in love comes after *falling.*
Pray you'll land on your feet.

Above all, *agapè* – when you forget
who you are and take someone's hand.

Ante

Our children are only a blueprint. We imagine their milky bodies
flickering in a sonogram. We unpack our cases. They're hiding

under our crisp bed in the hotel. The sun sinks into a cocktail glass.
Mouth the Spanish word for blood, think out loud: *there will be*

so many things to learn. Drink one guilty mouthful; let bubbles
fizz between your teeth. Mark this occasion of knowing in silence.

You no longer recognise the tilted face on the curve of your glass.

Christening

Mother is a swimming pool of voices,
    the wet limbs of children.
  You stare
    through mothers reflected
in training pool windows:
              flickering, mutable,
your see-through face among them.

You wait for a child.
Your name rises from water.

The Audience

Before I go back to myself,
kiss me. Right here, in this cinema.
Let it be nitrate.
Let it burn underwater.
Let all the actors talk themselves
into a neat ending. We'll applaud.

Kiss me before I slip
back into something uncomfortable.
Don't you prefer the dark?

Learning the Steps

Every Saturday, our dance teacher looks up
to God in the lightbulbs, and silently prays
our trainers will turn into red shoes. *Amen.*

We're not ballerinas. We're looping in circles
and getting nowhere, mostly anticlockwise,
making vines out of arms and legs.

We dance to learn about a part of ourselves
books can't teach; it's what our parents expect.
If we hop on a wrong note a bear will eat us.

We're learning the steps of old island lives:
hasapiko, kalamatiano, syrto; a dragging dance
where you're carried along by the wrists.

We leap like salmon, trying to catch scent of home,
as music pours through speakers like flood
and our bodies vibrate with the boom.

Still, there we go again, tripping up,
making shoddy Xs with feet that want
to place themselves on an invisible map.

Ferry

Natasha is sixteen, drunk on Flemish Beer.
She sobs and giggles, loudly threatens
to jump into the English Channel.

Roll your eyes. Comfort hungover Amy
who threw up outside the large window
of the hypermarché restaurant. Leave her.

Hang around with a walkman on deck.
Pretend you're in a pop video. Mime at grey.
Forget the rows of white crosses in Ypres.

Vow to get further than any of them.
Be different. Pause. Breathe in salted air.
Go back to the girls with sore heads.

Watch the milky light of England rise.
See everything in front of you, fogged.
Feel the land's pull, its terrible magnet.

Songbird

She flew in with a stolen heart. She had a vacant nest
where she didn't keep any letters to remind herself
who she really was. An unkempt roost was enough.
A snatch of bread. A shiny object to admire alone
with no value, only an unreflecting mirror of silver.

A girl trapped in lime.
She grew wings that were too heavy to lift.
learned her song. Sometimes I sense a flutter
of her trilling notes under my ribs.

You can't release that bird anywhere –
there's no country on any map for her to return.

The Distance

My family never got the hang of England,
arriving in London, scattering lives into flats,
hollering from balconies instead of olive groves.

It's my name being screamed over the estate.
My aunt wants me home for dinner, she's busy
tying mint into bouquets with yarn,

willing the stalks to dry in weak sunshine.
From the ground she looks besieged by foliage
with leaves and herbs growing from old cans

and emptied margarine tubs. My uncle's indoors,
persuading Babba to another shot of brandy,
the volume turned up on his satellite TV

with a band playing tsamiko for a wedding.
When neighbours complain he ignores them,
turning irritations into nimble dance steps,

a gurgle of B-flat clarinets to guide him.
I'll enter the room with a bag of school books,
curdling with embarrassment at his display.

Years later I throw open my windows to rain
knowing my aunt's echoes won't travel the distance,
I'm here, I say to water, *can't you shout any louder?*

My Stranger

hangs where the plaster cracked
and the ribs of the house show.
He's the only stranger I can afford,
a middle-aged man in a plaid shirt
smiling for an artist. Nothing to me,
but still I hang him in the hallway
and call him *Dad*. Of course, visitors
have doubts. I know they know
his hair's too light, the eyes too blue.
I win them over by recalling
our fishing holidays, how dad slit
the belly of a rainbow trout and out
slipped a diamond ring for me.
A perfect fit. Dad was handy.
He met my mother when she broke
down outside the Camden Palace,
and changed her tyre without a jack.
He made us a sherbet playhouse,
we licked its walls to nothingness.
He taught my brother harpsichord.
Now he's international. You may
have heard him on the radio.
That's a self-portrait. He never lived
to paint us all. 'What a terrible loss,'
visitors sigh. I lead them into
a living room and whisper, 'Yes.'

Choose Your Own Adventure

1

On your search for the grey-furred mountain gorillas
you come across the orc. Throw a die.
Your throw is impressive.
Cast him from the high-ledge
so he falls to his doom. Cock him a snook.
You have no choice but to return home.

Turn to **13**

13

Your family squabbles over stew.
They have the eloquence of swifts.
No one cares about how you defeated the orc,
it is the same life lived every day.
Father reminds you that your brothers and sisters
were married at your age (with proper jobs).
You can't even find a grey-furred mountain gorilla.

To feign a headache and go to your room turn to **25**.
To go out for the night turn to **75**.

75

In the inn of the monopods
you choose a double vodka shot.
Scylla buys the rounds
she blows poison in the men's ears.
You drink and drink from the vile chalice
that replenishes itself. Drink and drink
until you throw up. Charybdis
holds back your hair. A true friend.
If only the dance floor would stay still.

To go home in a taxi turn to **40**.
To seek the elegant stranger who'll take you
to Zizzi's and save you from this mess turn to **37**.

37

He's married. Go to **40**.

40

You wake up by the river of daggers
worghests and goblinoids lick your face.
The water tastes of dejection. The orc's orcish solicitor
has posted you a letter written in the strongest terms.

To pull the covers over your head turn to **25**.
That's it, there's no other option.

25

You dream. The wise wererat pulls out the cards.
Out of three possible endings you may choose only one:

The High Priestess of Speed Dating
The Page of Sorrow
The Magician (Reversed)

How to Survive a Disaster Movie

Stay away from landmarks.
Stay away from New York, Paris and London,
under no account visit San Francisco.
Own a dog. Do not get fat.
Have a child by your side, ideally an orphan.
Carry a tin-opener. Learn to appreciate
the taste of asphalt after fall-out.
Ensure your life skills are plot-dependent –
it's possible to kill zombies with a skewer
once used to spatchcock a quail.
Be the President of the United States.
Do not be the President of the United States.
Do not assume your head is safe
from the jaws of a Tyrannosaurus Rex.
Sweat. Let your huge muscles gleam.
If you must have sex, be quick.
Be attentive to the fluctuations of incidental music.
Lick your thumb and read the weather.
Ensure you're with the right survivors.
On the face of it, hold nothing dear.

The Vale

You're thirteen.

A girl is glassed in an alley
near home. Her webbed face
stays with you and her name
is on every pair of lips
in the lower school.
She must have done something bad
to get that. Violence. Justice.
Part of the scenery like weeds
or abandoned cars.

You're seventeen.

Afternoons you saunter home
from school, under skies
coloured like pencil-nibs.
You manage the weight
of 960 pages of Sociology
in your rucksack. A pop tune
is spinning in your head.

It's always like this, till one day
there's six of them. Waiting.
You've done nothing wrong.

All you know is that you must
get home, climb the stairwell,
only remember to breathe
after the latch has clicked shut.

One says, *she's only a girl*
and you're walking –
you just keep walking.

Mr. Alessi Cuts the Grass

There's a noise outside,
it sounds like a man is pushing
something larger than dreams
over concrete, or maybe
he's trying to make a garden
out of his life from whatever
comes to hand: flowers and rubble,
sorting out what's needed
from what isn't, willing
broken objects around him
to grow into something new.

I shake off my half-sleep
and shuffle to the window
to see Mr Alessi across the street
battling with his lawnmower.
It's only the clank of rusted metal
from a rattletrap machine,
but for a moment –

Not About Hollywood

I sit next to Uncle Tony in the waiting room
who says he'll be lucky to get six months

and can't be sure if it's his blood pressure
or the ghosts in his head that'll kill him.

He wears a jacket removed from a corpse
with his life savings stitched under tweed,

'So they don't get at it,' he whispers,
they being banks, governments, wives.

My mother's seen it all. I was born
into melodrama. But we're still here for him

the way a scratching post is there for a cat.
He talks. We listen to the silences.

Magazines find their way onto our laps
and we lose ourselves in other lives:

premieres, evening gowns, red carpets.
He gets up, humming something staccato.

His step falters. We tell him not to worry
as his name flashes in blood-red lights.

Gangsters

Bassetlaw men always talked coal
behind closed doors, away from kids.
I imagined them in pin-stripes
and trilbys in Working Men's clubs,
smoking, playing seven card stud.

My father might be a gangster.
I had to check so stayed up late
to see him back from the club
with a pack of poppets for me,
a beery kiss, tell-tale trace of cigar.

He said coal had no future,
he drifted from place to place:
Cottam, High Marnham, West Burton,
like bad men did in movies,
whistling, coin-flipping in bars,
a tommy gun in our Cortina's boot.

I was too young to understand
why my father wanted out.
We were public enemies on the run.
I'd reach up to his blackbird face,
press my lips on soot. We'd scram,
split, not knowing our crime.

Problems with the Idiom

It does not feel, as they say,
as if I'm *walking* into a brick wall.

No, forget that. I'm not *walking*
into it, I'm trying to *eat* a wall.

That's more difficult. It's easy
to *walk* into a wall, *eating* it isn't.

I try, and lance a brick.
The fork sparks a trail. To think

my teeth will suffer worse!
A *whole* brick wall. Where to start?

Where will it go? There is no
idiom in the English language

for *love is a brick wall people eat*.
The weight! My plate breaks in half.

The broken pieces remind me
of aspirin, maybe the moon.

The moon's a romantic image,
often swallowed whole.

Anna of The Fisheries

Not for the hungry who enter the shop
leaving fingerprints on everything,
or for her uncle, her tutting boss,
will she scrub the fryer's chrome
till it's a mirror for her forced smile.

Not for salt & vinegar tears over chips,
for a labourer's fish supper wrapped
in inky pages from a *Daily Mail*,
or for teddy boys in brothel creepers,
will she gather tips in a coffee jar.

Not for gossip with backcombed wives
will she wear her alchemist's overalls.
Home is seven days away on a ship.
Anna drops slabs of cod into bubbling oil
and waits for batter to turn into gold.

Yiayia's House

Nothing more than two rooms
painted white, with a smell of wheat
around the bedding. On hot nights
we sat on her old woven chairs
talking in the yard, nearly asleep.

Through an insistent *jurr jurr*
of crickets, Yiayia's voice was soft.
She'd bless her absent husband,
my grandfather. Her prayer mingled
with the fast wings of insects
gathered around the outdoor light;
its brightness keeping them out
from the house he built for her.

Fylingdales

Moors are god-peppered purple
and ghosts are everywhere.
We pass the Ministry of Secrets,
the land's sore thumb.
Its one-eyed radar
scours clouds for attack.
A Mayday – *save-me-save-me*
passes over fell-walkers,
all swinging arms and purpose.
Unheard whispers
disperse over a jagged
horizon.
                    Something quivers.

Esk, Derwent –
                    signs for water
with no water to be seen.
Cotton grass bows.

We breathe in
the bottle-green hardness
of silence.

Don vs. the Summer of Love

In '67 Don's cock of the walk, locker talk and cologne.
He struts through the Summer of Love all real estate
and military honours, dressed like a nutcracker.

Somewhere along the journey he meets Brianne –
barefoot under the honey locusts of Central Park.
It has rained. The grass is cool. Brianne can't stay.

She stares into the bark, *I'll always be moving; be moved*
someplace else. Brianne confuses Don. She offers him a daisy.
White tassels fall from her arms. She sews her own wings.

Don grows impatient. *Where the hell do you see yourself*
in fifty years time? Brianne says, *In heaven*. Don thinks, *Me too,*
bullion hotels, silk women; a big white boudoir of a nation.

Brianne strokes the petals losing their beauty to dusk.
She whispers, *Look at the ruined moon. One day I will be old*
and one day you will be old – but we won't be the same.

Role Model

Neither Thelma nor Louise, nor side-saddled
on a milk-white horse through Death Valley

nor a fashionista, a sweet-tooth for luxury
statement heels, a homicidal stiletto thing

nor Julie Andrews with a guitar, the whiskers
the kittens, the woman who's holy water

nor a mistress with a dozen married lovers
never showering alone, phone set on vibrate.

I'd like to be the woman next door
with a walk that says *I know where I'm going.*

Wearing Red

For Charlie

Old enough to no longer care,
a woman in a curtained room
lets dark jeans fall to her feet
then zips herself into a red dress
and everything it means, staring
at her brave twin in the mirror
who mouths back *'why not?'*

Later, red pours from bottles
and leaves kiss marks on glasses.
She realises how comfortable
redness feels. It's not a disguise.
It's her way of saying *'I'm here.'*

Ragtrade

My mother learnt young. Her hands
grew into the trade, feet worked pedals
from barefoot to heeled to slippered.

Always a delicate business, she knew
how much pressure was enough before
fabric might concertina into waste.

The machine was the first thing to go
after she left. Its bulky mystery a puzzle
we couldn't solve, much too big for us.

What's left of her trade is crammed
into rusting tins of cotton reels, needles
and wax, tools to make and renew.

I root around worthless silver bobbins,
pins and zips. She's somewhere in this mess
but I've lost her. Things have changed.

We learn to dispose of the easy to mend,
incapable of fixing tears and damage,
unable to stitch over our losses.

Aviary

Behind mesh are bodies and wings
coloured like expensive cocktails:
mojito birds, gin-blue weavers
daiquiri finches with twitchy heads.
The man who visits everyday
wears the drabness of a wren,
ignores a polite warning sign,
pushes bread through rusted wires.
He's grown the tongue of a bird,
speaks in a language of clicks
and whistles until they draw close.
They talk. He calls each one love.

The Horse

Everyone says I should get back on the horse.
I sneak up on her, but she's too quick,
she rams her hooves into my hoof-proof vest.
Too bad, horse. I may not be able to get back on you
but I know the score.

*

The horse is grazing in a field.
I have prepared complex equations
for getting back on horses. I nod at the farmer
who's seen others trying to saddle up.

*

It's early evening and meadow sweet.
There's a kind of light that drives poets crazy.
I pad over softly to my horse,
now at rest in her stable. I sing to her
with such tenderness even a stud would sigh.

*

Morning. Drizzle. Horse laughs.
I am a joke on many social networks.

*

Horse is my editor. Horse is Dustin Hoffman
in *All the President's Men. You wanna get back on me*
you're gonna have to do it my way, say her conker-coloured eyes.

She pours strong coffee, rests her hooves on the table.

*

Sweet horse, gentle horse
let me know your warmth – a touch
of your mane.

Darling horse, I wrote you a haiku.

*

As horses go I have had my fill of horses. There's nothing special about you. You're just like all the other horses in poems, let's face it you're no looker. See I snapped my pencil in two. Go neigh at the moon, Equestriana.

*

Horse is standing on my desk,
her snorts pure anger.

Say that again, horse, didn't understand,
My partner appears at the door, aghast.

No worries, private joke, I say.

*

It's on a Thursday I mount her.
I was out for bread and milk in town,
she was trotting along beside me.
So humble. She even buckled her knees
to make it easier.

Thank you, horse.
Bless your stirrups and your saddle.

Let me stay on.

Woman Running Alone

A woman who follows her own trail
and pounds pavements of unending cities,
past statues of forgotten men, fountains,
sticky sunshine pouring over tower blocks,
past gentrified basement windows
where wives hear the washing-up howl
between their hands, past suits on phones
and panda-eyed women in doorways
with faces that say *I know, I know – tell me
about it*; these streets where open hands
beg for more than is ever offered,
where someone's kid is a sleeping bag,
where the wolf-whistle becomes the wolf
and love's worn like musk aftershave,
where she forgets who she is: *Ms. Keep On,
Ms. Never-going-home,* neither running away
nor running toward anyone, wind-sifted,
letting the weather sing through her,
she who is different to her brothers.

The rhythm fills her with flight –
                    and her wings,
                        what wings she has –

Acknowledgements and Thanks

Some poems have been previously published in the following places: **Journals and magazines:** *Agenda, Ambit, Atrium, Black Bough, Coast to Coast to Coast, Harana, Litter, Magma, New Boots and Pantisocracies, New Walk, Poems in Which, Poetry Salzburg, Pratik, Stand, Strix, The Compass, The Interpreter's House, The Manchester Review, The North, The Rialto, The Warwick Review.*

Anthologies: 'Woman Running Alone': *The Result is What You See Today: Poems About Running,* ed. Ben Wilkinson, Kim Moore & Paul Deaton, (The Poetry Business, 2019).'The Horse': *Coming and Going: Poems for Journeys,* (HappenStance Press, 2019). 'Friday at the Moon': *One for The Road: An Anthology of Pubs and Poetry,* ed. Helen Mort and Stuart Maconie, (The Poetry Business, 2017). 'Learning the Steps': *The Emma Press Anthology of Dance,* (The Emma Press, 2015). 'Hypothetical': *The Poetry of Sex,* ed. Sophie Hannah, (Penguin, 2014). 'Anna of the Fisheries': *Cruising Down the Lane,* ed. Agnes Marton and Harriet Lawler, Moon and Mountain, (2013).

Competitions: Aurora Prize, Writing East Midlands (2017), judged by Penelope Shuttle. Commended for 'Songbird.' York Literature Festival Poetry Competition: Commended, judged by Carole Bromley, (2014) for 'Wearing Red.'

My thanks go out to all the editors who have published my work and to friends and family who have supported me over the years. A big thank you in particular to Kathy Bell, Nell Nelson, Josephine Corcoran, Martin Stannard, Roy Marshall, Liz Berry, Mark Anthony Owen, Matthew Stewart, WORD! Poetry Leicester, and all the team at Five Leaves Bookshop, Nottingham. A special thanks goes to the Creative Writing team at De Montfort University. I'm also indebted to John McCullough, Carrie Etter and Kathy Pimlott for their kind words. I would especially like to thank Jane Commane and Angela Hicken at Nine Arches Press for their support and believing in this manuscript. Most of all, lots of love to my family: to my parents, Jonathan, Rosie and Miranda. It would not have been possible to write these poems without you.